Tea Is A Time,
A Gracious Time

Tea Is A Time,
A Gracious Time

Bethelyn Sue Gadbow

To order additional copies of this book, contact:
Xlibris Corporation
1-888-795-4274
www.Xlibris.com
Orders@Xlibris.com
95951

FOREWARD

GRACE

Disposition to or an act or instance of kindness,

special favor, charming, trait of accomplishment

—a quality or state of being considerate or thoughtful

—given of charm and beauty.

GRACEFUL

Displaying grace in form or action.

GRACIOUS

Marked by tact and delicacy—characterized

by charm, good taste and generosity.

Do not let your adornment be merely outward . . . .

rather let it be the hidden person of the

heart, with the incorruptible beauty of a

gentle and quiet spirit, which is precious

in the sight of God.

I Peter 3:4 NKJV

TEA begins in the heart of a little girl.

Somewhere. I don't know just where. She

doesn't know where—

but there it is.

See her?

She's been in the closet.

Her Mother's dress is one she

thinks is special and just her color. It is held up,

somewhat, with a belt. Her high heeled shoes cause

her to wobble as she walks, but that is okay.

The gloves are a little or a lot

too long in the fingers.

She prefers the hat to have a large brim

and a veil.

She has invited her special friends.

There are Teddy Jane and Bunny Jane and

her doll Sarah Jane.

(She likes the name, Jane.)

They are all on their best behavior and

have on their finest clothes.

She has seated her guests at the tea table. The

cloth is pretty. At least she thinks it is.

The flowers are plastic or the bouquet

may be made of dandelions from the yard.

The candle is quite possibly from the" powder room",

which mother doesn't know she has, or the citronella

one from the patio.

The tea set is designer from Woolworth,

(These days they would be collectibles.)

or from

Walmart.

Her guests are very demure. They don't raise

their voices. They talk only in hushed tones.

They don't talk about others.

They are so thankful to be together.

They are so special to each other.

Occasionally the little girl will pass the tea sweets

and insist that Jane have another. And Sarah Jane

may need some more tea.

"More lemon?" "Two sugar cubes or one?"

She is serving the finest of fare.

Whatever she thinks her guest would like

and as light as air.

How peaceful—this tea time.

No rush.

No interruptions.

Just a special little girl with her special

little friends

having a special time at TEA.

When they are finished, the dishes will be

replaced on the shelf,

the guests back on the bed,

and the clothes back in the closet, until the

next time.

Are they still there?

Why not get them out again?

Why not experience the special and intimate

feeling of TEA again.

PREFACE

Giving or inviting

someone to TEA involves

more than a cup of Oolong or Earl Grey.

It doesn't have to involve tea to drink.

Rather, it is a time that is shared with someone special.

Many a friend or neighbor has invited or been invited

over for a cup of coffee, tea, or soft

drink. Maybe some cookies or sweet rolls will be shared.

But this is not TEA.

TEA is more than sharing food,

discussing news, or planning.

It is a time of sharing with and giving of

yourself to and for another.

It is a special time between those who are sharing

the moment.

This book is written to help you experience
giving a special kind of hospitality called TEA.
I want to help you incorporate the words
defined at the beginning into your hospitality.
You may say, "I'm not a graceful person".
Well, no one has ever accused me of being gracious
about anything either. Being gracious has very
little to do with personality or the fact that you
may be down-right clutsy.
It has to do with giving yourself in hospitality
and letting your own personality show through.
So you are not Victorian or soft spoken. So you don't
have all the social graces of a Southern Belle.
So, be gracious in your way. Gracefulness
is not in outer beauty but in inner beauty that
radiates to those around you because you
care, because you have a spirit of generosity,
not necessarily in things but in giving of
yourself. Not in episodes of pretense
but in quiet, unassuming consistency.
So, a TEA can be a gracious time because
a gracious woman
invites, prepares, and gives
to another.

TEA IS A TIME . . . . A GRACIOUS TIME

A time of a special kind.

A time for two or three or more
who are invited through your door.

A time for family or friend
a little of yourself to spend.

A time to share
and show you care.

A time of little or much
when time stands still and emotions touch.

A time of grand or simple things
can a special closeness bring.

TEA is a gift to you from me.
You are special—don't you see?

"A time of a special kind . . ."

Times of gracious hospitality have become
almost non-existant in this world of
hurry and worry.
There seems to be no time, no place,
to set aside everyday
hustle and bustle
and find and enjoy the world of "gracious".

Graciousness is not always easy.
It may take time to develop.
It may not come natural,
but it is worth the effort.
Real giving of yourself, no matter the setting,
the place or the expense
is true graciousness.

So invite a special person or persons for TEA.
Oh, this is not one of those times
when everyone brings something
and the neighbors,
or the church
are discussed,
or plans for next year's bazaar are made.
It is a time when giving
"because I want to" is the priority.
Nothing is expected in return.

<u>"A time for two or three or more</u>
<u>who are invited through your door."</u>

The important word is "invited".
TEA is not happenstance. It is not a drop-in thing.
Who to invite?
The president of my club? Probably not.
Someone I want to impress? Absolutely not.
Someone I want to pour out my problems to? Certainly not.
Someone I want to do something special for. Sure.
Start there. You can invite one or several.
It doesn't matter.
Of course, the number would be determined by
how many you can manage in your home.
TEA does not have to be done in your home,
although that is very special.
You can choose from some of the tea rooms
that are in your area.
Just be sure
to choose a place that will not detract
from what you want to convey to
the special person or persons.
Maybe somewhere private,
away from distractions.
Whether it is in your home or away
graciousness is found in the intent.
Sure, you can invite someone over for dinner
or take them out, and you may be able to say
"You are special"
in this setting,
but TEA is very personal and focused.

<u>"A time for family or friend,</u>

<u>a little of yourself to spend.</u>"

Our world is so busy. You will agree with that.
Everyone has a least one
job whether it is for salary or volunteer.
Often we hear, "I don't have time." Really!
Time is too short for us not to take time to express,
"You are special to me."
We spend many hours discussing others.
How much time and energy do
we spend to say, "Thank you" or "I care".
Giving of things has taken the place
of giving of self,
but which is more meaningful?
Cost is not the worth of the gift.
A gracious time may be more
meaningful than an expensive gift.
Things may be forgotten,
but special times will remain with us forever.
I'm sure you can remember, as can I,
someone who did something that said
"You are special"
and that meant more than any gift.
We may choose to
forget bad times but special times
we hold close to our hearts.

"A time to share . . . and show you I care."

Make your TEA a relating time.

Oh, I realize if you give of yourself

in this way,

you may become the listener,

the confidante.

It may be a time when the giver says,

"You gave to me. I want to give to you.

I want to show you I care. "

Make your TEA an intimate time.

"Let me give to you."

Let me do for you."

These are the desires of a

gracious woman in a gracious time.

"A time of little or much
when minutes stand still and emotions touch."

TEA is not a menu.
Look at the little girl who has TEA with her teddy bear
and friends.
Fancy foods? I don't believe so.
Probably peanut butter and crackers and Koolaid
or lemonade.
What is the important thing?
That they are together.
That they are sharing.
Who knows, maybe the plate has
paper cookies and the cup is empty.

TEA can include as little as some kind of sweet treat
or sandwich and a drink.
(By the way, your special person may not like
to drink tea in any way it can be fixed.)
Multiple courses that include a meat dish is called
"High Tea".

It is time together without restrictions
or rushing
that is the important ingredient of TEA.

"<u>A time of grand or simple things</u>

<u>can a special closeness bring</u>."

TEA can be served with formal china, sterling or gold plate,

silver tea service, soft music,

white tea cloth and napkins.

It can be served indoors in the

dining room, a study or any place that is pretty and cozy.

You may use fancy or plain dishes.

It really doesn't matter.

Dishes do not need to match.

Sterling and gold can be used together

but

dishes should be complimentary.

You may choose to use less formal dishes
and accessories.
It may be that" formal" is not your thing.
You may not feel comfortable with what you
see as
"fluff".
It is the verbal and noverbal communication that is the
special part of all that you are doing.
Don't get lost in doing something that makes you
ill at ease.

The effort made to give a TEA brings the participants
closer because of the
graciousness
of the giver.

"<u>TEA is a gift to you from me.</u>
<u>You are special-Don't you see!</u>"

View the TEA that you are planning
as a gift.
Spend time and plan it well
just as you would if it were a special
gift in a box.
A gift that you thought about
and carefully wrapped.
Now you wait with anticipation as the
gift
is given.

Giving of yourself is the best gift
you can give.
Give it with grace not pretense.
Be real.
Give in the spirit of generosity.

TEA is a time—a place
for the heart and mind to be quiet
and at peace.

Let me take you away to TEA.
Away from turmoil to quiet.

Thee and me,
together at
TEA

OCCASIONS

One of the most special things about TEA is that
you can use almost any occasion to
express graciousness.

Anniversaries are a special time for couples,
couples and friends,
or
couples and families.
Of course, the key to making this a personal time is in
the group that is invited.
Be sure that any friends that are invited are close
so that the time can be special.
The number is not important. The closeness of
the group is. Live music is a nice added touch
if it can be arranged, but soft taped music is also nice.

Holidays are great times to be
gracious.

How about Christmas?
The season is in itself a "giving time".
It is a natural time for getting together.
It is the season for parties like no
other season.
This setting and the thoughts of
Christmas
make it easy to express your feelings.
You can invite a large group
or several small groups.
The house is decorated and festive.
The candles are lit.
Special food is ready.
Your guest complete the picture.

Other holidays
New Years,
Valentine's Day,
Easter.
You pick.

Birthday TEAs are usually a little
more light-hearted.
Add your touch
to the occasion to make it
special,
not just another birthday party.
After all,
if you are giving or arranging the
TEA, you are also the director and the
one who is the hostess.
This doesn't have to be
expensive,
but,
it does need to be well planned.

Bridal, wedding, and baby showers
are great times for TEAs.
They are always special with the added
planning that goes into TEA.
Just mentioning that it is a
TEA
almost always sets the
atmosphere of something
special.

TEAs for children are some of the most
special times.
Put out the same effort for the
youngsters
as you do for the
adults.
You will be surprised how they move into
the mood of a gracious time.
Change the menu to foods that they will like.
Try some cold or warm apple juice or apple cider
in their cups if they don't want
to try any kind of tea.
Some of the fruit flavored teas might
go well for children.

All little girls will love fancy dishes,

cups and saucers.

Don't think it is necessary to

use plastic or styrofoam.

They cannot learn the joy of finer things

if they never get to experience them.

Let them learn.

If you are worried about breakage of fine pieces,

let them use less expensive but

beautiful pieces. There are lots of

beautiful ones.

Four years old is not

too young if the TEA is fairly short

in time

and Mom is with them.

Five years old is not too early

if you are careful with the time.

No more than three or

four at a time will work,

but more may mean

a loss of control,.

and will not be a learning

experience.

TEA for teen-agers can be great fun.

They hear about these
occasions
and are willing to learn,
dress up clothes and all.
They may even try tea for you.
Always have an alternative.
They will feel very special and
that is what we want them to feel.
They will not learn to be gracious unless
they see it and experience it

A TEA for a lady and her friends or women
who are a part of a special group can
be greatly appreciated by
those who are honored.
You may want to say
"Thank you"
to a special group of teachers
or secretaries.
The group might be your sisters
or your
aunts.
Are they special to you?
Then give a TEA in
their honor.
If they leave feeling they are special,
you have accomplished your goal.
The adage, "It is more blessed to give
than to receive", is true.
But more than that, you receive as well
as the other person
when you give.
They may feel special, but you have
received joy in doing and giving.

Mother and daughter TEAs.

How special.

Little girls and their mothers-

Older girls and their mother-

Even older daughters with their mothers.

Such a special time that you can say,

"I love you" or Thank you".

Never let these times slip into

everyday talk.

You can do that over the telephone.

Remember, you have a purpose.

Don't lose sight of it.

Don't let a time like this slip

by

unfulfilled.

You may not get the chance

later.

The next group of occasions

is what I call,

"Just because".

Maybe it is or is not Valentine's Day,

a birthday, an anniversary, or

a holiday.

It is certainly okay to express your

feeling

any day of the year.

Your special feelings may not want

to wait for a special day

to be expressed.

Someone may need encouragement today.

Someone may need

your special gift today.

Open your eyes and your mind.

There are many people that are special to you.

Take time, now, to express your

feelings.

A time to do this later may be

lost before you get it done.

Those "too late" experiences are sometimes

tragic.

When you give or arrange a

TEA,

really, you are the recipient of pleasure.

Giving to and for others has great

rewards.

These are the rewards of a

gracious

woman.

INVITATIONS

Invitations should be complimentary of
the occasion.
They don't have to be expensive,
although they can be.
They can be hand drawn.
They can be done on a computer
(if you are a computer-whiz, which I
am not).

Some of the most special ones are

hand drawn pictures.

Why?

Because you made it.

The content of the invitation should set up

the feeling of

anticipation.

You may need to include such words as

"elegant" or "casual" if you

want to convey a dress preference.

However, if your guest arrive in

the wrong attire—

so what?

You still think they are special.

Don't make a big deal of it.

If they ask,

be specific.

If they don't ask and you don't tell them,

then dress conservatively so they

are not

uncomfortable.

Invitations can be mailed or
delivered by hand.
Think of a unique way to deliver it.
Maybe a simple flower and the
invitation
on a desk when the person arrives for work,
or on the table when they come
home from
shopping.
You think of something special.
You may say,
"I can't".
I say,
"You can".
Try it.
It will get easier with practice.

PLACES

Where do you have TEA?

Anywhere.

Some of the places will depend on

the number of people involved.

Dining rooms lend themselves to formal

TEAs.

But you can have a formal TEA in almost

any room or in the yard.

A formal TEA depends on the way it is

served

rather than on the place.

Formal TEAs will demand

elegant dishes,

candles,

silver,

and flowers.

Soft music is special if it can be arranged.

Dens or kitchens or anywhere a simple table
can be set would be a great
place
for less formal TEAs.

What about TEA in the home of that special person
that cannot get out?
Even when served in a bedroom,
it can be special
because of the people who are
together.

You might want to unpack your TEA
from a picnic basket
in the park.
My mother would take my
sister and me to a school
yard
when we were little girls.
The menu was Ritz crackers and
peanut butter.
We had lemonade to drink
but we were at TEA
with Mother.
Adults love the
special freshness
of outside activities.
Bring your good cups, saucers, and
plates.
This is a special situation.

TEAs that are held out of doors
are very special.
Patios, decks, porches, or
the yard
can be very nice. They can be elegant if
planned well.
Votive candles can be used instead of tapers
if the wind is a problem.
If you should choose the out of doors,
be sure to do
whatever is necessary
to control any
bothersome insects.
Gracious does not include
swatting these kinds of
intruders.
Also, be sure you have an
alternate plan in case of
inclement weather.

If you find you are unable to serve

TEA in your home, there

are Tea Rooms

that can provide these very

special and private times.

It doesn't mean

you care less

or that the TEA would be

less special if you make

these kinds of arrangements.

Just be sure you

look around till you find the best place.

SETTINGS

Formal TEAs will require your best china,

silver or gold table service.

(Good stainless can

be used as well.)

Silver or china tea pots,

crystal, flowers

and candles will help

the appearance of your table.

All white cloths and napkins can be

used.

However, don't be afraid to use colored

crystal or colored cloths and napkins.

If well coordinated, these

can be as elegant as

all white.

You can use unmatched china

and silver and gold on the

same table, as long

as they compliment each other.

Candles and flowers

are a must,

but should be arranged so a person

doesn't have to dodge or peer around them

to feel they are sharing with the other person

or persons.

Informal TEAs can include more
casual settings.
Checkered or floral cloths or
napkins are good.
Wild, dried, or silk flowers
and less formal
candles can
add a touch of color and pull
the appearance of your table together.

Holidays, special seasons, and special days
can give you unending opportunities
to show your creativity.

TEAs for children and young people can
open up all kinds of varieties to try.

MENUS

The following are only sample menus,

all of which have five courses.

There can be more or less.

You decide.

You can mix and match these recipes

or

add some things of your own.

Remember,

"High Tea"

means that a meat dish is included.

Some of the main keys to successful teas is

planning well and starting early,

so you don't

become a disaster while you are

preparing for your special time.

Those who attend will not appreciate

you more if you are too tired

to be gracious.

"Gracious" never says,

"I have killed myself to do this for you".

1.

Butter-swirl cake and Poppyseed bread
with
Strawberry-honey butter

Cucumber and cream cheese sandwiches
on mini rye slices

English muffins or scones with
Raspberry Jam

Chicken salad with
Honey-wheatberry rolls

Carrot Cookie
with
Cream cheese frosting

2.

Butter-swirl cake and Banana-nut bread
with
Strawberry-honey butter

———————

Apple slices with caramel dip

———————

English muffins or scones

———————

Ham, turkey and cheese croussant
with
Chips and pickle spears

———————

Chocolate pudding

3.

(can be used as a diabetic menu
by using diabetic recipes
in the following pages)

Assorted crackers with cream-cheese ball

———————

Cucumber sandwiches with cream cheese
on mini rye

———————

Mixed green salad with
red wine
or
raspberry
vinegarette

———————

Baked chicken breast
with
apple slices
and
orange sauce

———————

Cream cheese soufflé with
Cool whip
and
almond topping

4.

Fruit bread of
any kind
with
Spun-honey butter

———————

Salmon and cream cheese
sandwich
on
pumbernickel bread

———————

Fruit salad

———————

Chicken and cream corn crepes
with
Brown sugar and honey sauce
and
Sugar peas
with
Honey wheat-berry rolls

Coconut sherbet balls

Other courses to choose from:

    Meats:

        Smoked turkey and wild rice salad

        Turkey and fruit salad

        Crepes with ham and pineapple

        Crepes with cream corn and chicken

        Layered sandwiches

Breads or cakes:

    Any fruit bread that is your favorite can be
        used for one of the first courses.

    There are many frozen specialty doughs or
        boxed bread mixes if you don't want
        to start from scratch.

Desserts:

    Pound cake with pineapple sauce.

    Sherbet balls rolled in shredded coconut.

    Whatever you serve, remember to keep the
        servings small if you are going to
        serve five courses.

RECIPES

Teas—The Drink

All tea comes from the same leaf of an evergreen bush.

Differences in teas are caused by

how they are processed.

There are three basic types of teas:

Black

Green

Oolong

Black Teas produce a rich and hearty brew

that is very popular in this country.

Some of them are: Assam: Most often used in blends

and is rich in color, and strong and full-bodied

and is loved for morning pick-me-ups.

Ceylon: Used mostly in blends and is also

a strong and rich tea.

Darjeeling: A very expensive tea, mostly used

in blends.

Known as the "champagne of teas".

Famous for its fruity bouquet and light

full-bodied taste.

Earl Grey: A blend of black teas scented with oil

of bergamot, a citrus fruit. A very

fragrant, full-bodied tea.

Green Teas produce a very delicate brew that is very
light in color. Mothers have used green tea for
many years for upset stomach.

Two of them are:

> Gunpowder: A clear aromatic brew, which
> can sometimes be bitter.
> Hyson: A clear, light, gentle brew that
> leans toward being bitter or sharp.

Oolong Teas are a blend of black and green teas.
The brew produced is lighter in both flavor and color.

Three of them are:

> China Oolong: A light tea with
> a lovely fragrance.
> Formosa Oolong: An amber-colored
> tea, delicate in taste and
> considered to be the best
> of the Oolong teas.
> Mainland Oolong: A delicate Chinese
> tea with a wonderful aroma,
> sometimes scented with
> flowers.

For many years the Chinese have flavored their
teas with all kinds of spices, herbs, and fruits.
You will find many of them on the market. You
should try them all, and then decide your favorite.
Tea can be made by the cup or the pot.
Just remember that steeping them too long may
cause them to be bitter.

Chicken Salad

Boiled chicken breast—chopped (1 large chicken
breast will be enough for 3 servings)
Chopped celery
Chopped pecans
Chopped Granny Smith apples (unpeeled)
Chopped red Delicious or Jonathon apples
(unpeeled)
Chopped green onions (small amount)
Salt and Pepper to taste
Mayonnaise or salad dressing
Leaf lettuce

This can be made ahead except for chopped
apples and onions. Amounts are not
included in the recipe. You can use as much
or as little of the ingredients
according to your taste.

Cream cheese balls

8 oz. pkg. cream-softened
Add: Salt and pepper, Parsley flakes, Chives, Finely
chopped green onions, Chopped pecans, and
Rosemary leaves. The green onions are a must
to keep it from tasting bland. The rosemary
leaves will give it a distinctive taste. Make them
ahead and freeze.

Turkey Breast and Fruit Salad

> Baked and chopped turkey breast
> Chopped celery
> Chopped, dried dates
> Chopped walnuts or pecans
> Chopped and drained Mandarin oranges
> Cream cheese and Cool Whip dressing
> Leaf lettuce

Smoked Turkey and Wild Rice Salad

> Cooked and cooled brown rice (do not overcook)
> Cooked and cooled wild rice (do not overcook)
> Mandarin orange slices
> Chopped, unpeeled granny apples
> Chopped, unpeeled red Delicious or Jonathon apples
> Raisins
> Chopped pecans or walnuts
> Red wine and raspberry vinaigrette
> or Cool Whip and marshmallow cream dressing
> Leaf lettuce
> Let your guests layer this salad on leaf lettuce and the
> rice.

Orange Sauce

12 oz. frozen orange juice concentrate
12 oz. Cool Whip (use low-fat and low sugar for
diabetic)
1/2 pkg. French Vanilla instant pudding (use low-fat and
sugar-free for diabetics)
Margarine
    Stir pudding into Cool Whip
    Stir Cool Whip mixture into orange juice
    Heat over medium heat until thickened.
    Do not boil.
Stir in margarine just before serving.
    This will give it a smooth texture.
    It can be made ahead and then be
    reheated, but save the margerine
    till just before serving.

You will like this sauce so well that you will find
all kinds of things to put it on. It can be used as
a dressing for the Chicken Salad and Turkey
Breast Salad instead of mayonnaise for diabetics.
Just drizzle it on.

Pineapple Sauce

Follow directions for orange sauce using
crushed pineapple.
(Use "In it's own juice" for diabetics.)

Cream Cheese Souffle (very good for diabetics)

8 oz. cream cheese, room temperature
4 eggs—separated
12 pkg. Equal (don't use Sweet and Low)
Preheat oven to 350 degrees. If your oven cooks
hot, you will need to lower degrees to 325.
Cream the cheese with egg yolks till smooth.
Add sugar substitute. Beat egg whites until stiff,
but not dry. Fold cheese mixture into stiff egg
whites. Be careful not to break down egg whites.
Spray pie pan (not glass) generously with Pam
and pour in entire mixture. Place pan on cookie
sheet and bake.
Bake about 15 to 20 minutes.
(Depends on your oven.)

Bake until the top is dry and just beginning to
brown. Cool and serve with Cool Whip or
whipping cream. Sometimes your guest will
think it has a lemon taste. Other times it may
have an orange flavor. The secret is in the
brand of cream cheese.

Carrot Cookies

These are great. Everyone will want the
recipe. They make a cookie any size you want.
Any left over dough can be rolled in waxed paper
and frozen till you need it again. This way your
cookies will always be fresh baked. Just slice
what you need for the next cookies.

Follow directions for any carrot cake mix except
leave out the water. Batter will be stiff. Using a
tablespoon, drop dough on cookie sheet leaving
plenty of room between. Only one cookie per
person will be plenty. Frost with cream cheese
frosting and top with pecan half.
Any flavor cake mix can be used this way.
Chocolate, lemon, spice, and German chocolate are
all great
to make.

Butter-Swirl Cake

1 box Duncan Hines Butter Cake Mix
1/2 cup Wesson Oil
4 eggs
1/2 pint sour cream
1 cup pecans
2 Tbsp. brown sugar
2 tsp. cinnamon

Grease and sugar bundt or cake pan
Alternate layers of batter and brown
sugar, cinnamon, and pecan mixture.
Bake at 350 degrees for 60 minutes

Sweet Lemon Scones

    2 cups all-purpose flour
    1 Tbsp. salt
    4 Tbsp. sugar
    1 Tbsp. baking powder
    3 1/2 Tbsp. butter
    1 8 oz. carton low fat lemon yogurt
    2 eggs separated
    1 tsp, grated lemon peel
    3 Tbsp. heavy cream

Preheat oven to 425 degrees. Stir together
flour, salt, sugar, and baking powder. Using
a pastry blender, cut butter into flour mixture
until it resembles coarse crumbs. Stir together
the lemon yogurt, egg yolks, and lemon peel.
Add to the flour mixture and stir lightly with a
a fork. Add cream 1 Tbsp, at at time until
dough begins to clump together. Gather dough
on lightly floured surface and knead just three
or four times or until the dough holds together. (Do
not overwork.) Pat dough into a rectangle about 3/4 inch
thick and cut with 2-inch round cookie cutter. Place
scones on ungreased cookie sheet and brush tops with
beaten egg whites. Bake for 10 minutes or until
light brown. Serve warm. This recipe makes 16 scones.
Scones can be frozen before baking. Place on cookie
sheet in freezer until firm, then put in plastic bag and
keep frozen until ready to bake. Add just a few minutes
to the baking time.

Basic Scones

> 2 cups flour
> 1 Tbsp. baking powder
> 2 Tbsp. sugar
> 1/2 tsp. salt
> 6 Tbsp. butter
> 1/2 cup buttermilk
> 1 egg, lightly beaten

Mix dry ingredients. Cut in 6 Tbsp, butter until mixture resembles coarse cornmeal. Make a well in the center and pour in buttermilk. If you don't have buttermilk, use regular milk. Mix until dough clings together and is a bit sticky. Do not over mix. Turn out dough onto a floured surface and shape into a 6-to-8 inch round about 1 1/2 inches thick. Quickly cut into pie wedges or use a large round biscuit cutter to cut circles. The secret of tender scones is a minimum of handling. Place on ungreased cookie sheet, being sure the sides of scones do not touch each other. Brush with egg for a shiny, beautiful brown scone. Bake at 425 degrees for 10 to 20 minutes, or until light brown.

Scones are easy to make but packaged scone mix can also give you great results. Try adding some extras such as cut-up apples, cinnamon, apricots, chocolate chips or various flavorings.

Crepes

1 cup milk
1/2 cup water
2 eggs
2 Tbsp. butter, melted
2 Tbsp. vegetable oil
1 cup all purpose flour
1/4 tsp. salt

Combine all ingredients in mixing bowl.
Blend until smooth. Cover and set
aside at room temperature for 30 minutes.
Heat pan (a 7 inch skillet is a perfect size)
until butter sizzles or oil is hot. Add 2 Tbsp.
of the batter. Immediately tilt pan from
side to side so that batter covers the bottom
of the pan. Cook abut 1 1/2 minutes or until
crepe is lightly browned on one side. Turn
out onto a paper towel. Repeat with remaining
batter.

Crepes freeze well. To freeze, stack crepes,
separating them with layers of waxed paper.
Wrap stack in a moisture-proof bag. Thaw
one hour before using. Sprinkle with powered
sugar if using for dessert crepes.

Apricot Bread

    1 cup dried, chopped apricots
    1 cup granulated sugar
    2 Tbsp. Crisco
    1 egg, well beaten
    1/4 cup granulated sugar
    1 cup orange juice
    2 cups sifted flour
    2 tsp, baking powder
    1/2 tsp, soda
    1 tsp. salt
    1 cup chopped nuts

Soak dried apricots for 20 minutes. Meanwhile cream together 1 cup sugar, shortening, and egg. Stir in 1/4 cup sugar and 1/2 cup orange juice. Add dry ingredients and blend well. Drain apricots and stir apricots and nuts into batter. Bake in greased and floured loaf pan at 350 degrees for 65 minutes.

Wild Rice Soup

6 Tbsp. butter
1 Tbsp, minced onion
1/2 cup flour
3 cups chicken broth
2 cups cooked wild rice
1/3 cup minced ham
1/2 cup finely grated carrots
3 Tbsp. chopped or sliced almonds
1/2 tsp. salt
1 cup half and half
minced chives

Melt butter in sauce pan. Saute onions until
tender. Blend in flour. Gradually add broth.
Cook, stirring constantly until mix comes to
a boil. Boil 1 minute. Stir in rice, ham, carrots,
almonds and salt.

Simmer about 5 minutes. Blend in half and
half. Heat to serving temperature. Garnish
with parsley and chives.

Fruit Cobbler Dessert

Spray 9x12 cake pan with Pam.
Layer in cake pan, one on top of the other:

1 large can crushed pineapple
1 can cherry pie filling
1 cup chopped nuts
2 sticks margarine (cut and lay on top)

Sprinkle white or yellow cake mix
to cover the top. It will not take all
the cake mix. Use just enough to
cover.

Bake at 350 degrees for 1 hour. The margarine
will bubble up through the cake mix and make a
light crust. If you find this is too sweet, use
"In it's own juice" pineapple. This will help
cut the sweetness without losing the flavor.
(This is what I use.)
This dessert can still be in the oven while
you are serving your meal. Top with whipping
cream or ice cream.
Use any kind of pie filling such as peach,
apricot or apple, but always use the pineapple.

Fresh Apple Pound Cake with Black Walnuts

1 1/2 cups vegetable oil
2 cups sugar
3 eggs
Whip above three ingredients in mixing bowl for
three minutes.
In another bowl add: 3 cups sifted flour

1 tsp. salt
1 tsp. soda
1 tsp, cinnamon
1 tsp, vanilla

Sift dry ingredients together and add to first
mixture. Hold vanilla and mix to creamed
ingredients last. By hand add 1 cup diced
apples (peeled). Bake in greased Bundt
pan at 350 degrees for 1 hour and 25 minutes.
Let cook and remove from pan. This cake will
be better after two to three days. A good
make ahead dessert.

Butter Almond Chocolate Cake

    1/4 cup chopped blanched almonds
    3 Tbsp. Butter 1/2 cup sugar
    2 egg white
    2 tbsp Vanilla
    ½ C milk
    1 tsp salt
    2 cups Cool Whip
    1 9x12inch chocolate cake

Sautee nuts in butter in sauce pan until golden.
(Reserve 1/4 cup for garnish)
Add sugar, milk, egg yolks, and salt to
remaining nuts in sauce pan. ~.~
Stir over medium heat to boiling. Simmer 1 minute
or until lightly thickened. Add vanilla. Chill.
Beat egg whites until stiff. Fold in chilled
mixture, then Cool Whip.
Line 9x12 inch (bottom and sides) with
waxed paper or foil. Pour cream mixture into
pan and freeze for at least 4 hours-.
When ready to serve, split cake layer, making
2 thin layers. Place on serving plate.
Unmold the frozen mixture layer and
place onto 1 cake layer.
Top with second cake layer.
Sprinkle powdered sugar over top.
(You can use a paper doile to pattern
the powdered sugar if you like.)
Add almond garnish
This is a great make-ahead dessert. You can layer and
finish your dessert just before serving or you can finish it
and replace it in the freezer till you are ready to cut it. A
few minutes at room temperature will make it ready to
serve.

Mini Fruitcakes

1 pound red candied cherries, halved
3 oz. green candied cherries, halved
1 pound candied pineapple, cut into pieces,
1/2 pound pitted dates, chopped
1/2 pound golden raisins, 1 pound pecan pieces
1/4 cup all-purpose flour, for dredging fruits and nuts
1/4 cup (1/2 stick) butter, softened
3/4 cup firmly packed brown sugar, 2eggs
2 cups all-purpose flour, 1 1/2 tsp, baking soda
1 Tbsp, milk
1/2 cup peach brandy (most of the time I use rum)

(If you don't care for the different candied fruits, use
the kinds you like, keeping the total amounts the same.
If you choose, use chopped apricots and dates instead
of the other candied Iruits.)
In large mixing bowl, dredge fruits and nuts with 1/4 cup flour.
In a separate bowl with electric mixer on medium speed,
beat butter and brown sugar until fluffy. Add eggs and
mix well. Sift together 2 cups flour and baking soda. Add
flour mixture to butter mixture and mix. Add milk and
brandy (rum) and mix well. Add batter to dredged fruit and nuts.
Mix well. Batter will be very stiff. This dough is more fruit
than batter. Drop dough by Tbsps, onto well-greased
cookie sheet. Add 1/2 red candied cheery to top as
decoration
and bake at 275 degrees for 18—20 minutes or until
almost no imprint remains when touched lightly. Yields 9 dozen
bite-size cakes. If you choose, use little candy papers and place
in mini cupcake pan. Store in air-tight tin or plastic
container.
These are wonderful. They keep well. Easy to mail. Make
enough to last the entire holiday season.

Lacy Oatmeal Cookies

    I stick margarine-melted
    Add 3/4 cup white sugar
    Add 1/4 cup brown sugar
    Stir in:
    1 cup Quick Oats and 3 level Tbsp. flour
    Add 1 tsp, baking powder and pinch of salt.
    Add 1 tsp. vanilla
    Add 1 unbeaten egg.

Line baking sheets with foil. Spray foil
generously with vegetable oil cooking spray.
Drop batter by teaspoonful onto prepared
baking sheet, spacing 2 1/2 inches apart. Cookies
will spread. Bake cookies until golden, about 14 minutes
at 325 degrees. Remove from oven and slide
foil off sheet onto work surface. Cool cookies till
firm, about 5 minutes. Peel cookies off foil. Cool
completely on racks. You can wipe off, respray, and
reuse foil. Store in air-tight container.

Cream Scones

2 cups sifted cake flour
1/3 cup sugar
2 tsp. double acting baking powder
3/4 tsp, salt
5 1/2 Tbsp. butter
2 egg yolks
1/3 cup light cream
1/2 cup raisins (optional)
1 Tbsp. egg white
sugar for topping

Add sugar, baking powder and salt to sifted flour, then
sift mixture. Cut in butter. Gently beat together egg yolks
and cream, and combine with flour mixture. Add raisins
and
stir until soft dough is formed. Turn onto lightly floured
board and knead 20 times. Pat dough into a round at least
1/2 inch thick. With a 2 inch round cookie cutter, make as
many rounds as possible and place on ungreased cookie
sheet. Brush tops with lightly beaten egg white and
sprinkle with sugar. Bake for 10 minutes in 450 degree oven.
Scones should be golden brown on top. Serve with jam or
any whipped cream will do. Makes 1 dozen.

Lemon Curd

> 1 1/3 cups sugar
> 4 eggs
> Juice of 4 lemons
> (approximately 1/2 cup)
> 12 Tbsp, unsalted butter
> Grated rind of 2 lemons (optional)

Beat sugar and eggs until light and fluffy. Blend
with lemon juice. Pour mixture into saucepan and
heat over low heat until hot. Add butter, 1 Tbsp. at
a time, until completely melted and blended. Raise
the heat to medium and cook till thick. Stir well as
it thickens to prevent sticking and burning. Fold
in the rind. Cool until ready to serve with warm scones.

Personal Thoughts

My desire to give TEAs grew out of many years of entertaining as a pastor's wife. (I enjoyed it even before I had a dishwasher.) When my husband accepted a different position in our church structure, I no longer had those opportunities.

No longer could I serve a 24 person sit-down dinner. So I asked myself what I could do to take its place. I decided to become involved in small, very personal TEAs.

The first TEA I gave was for my sister, my only sister, my twin sister. I made her a "verandah" dress and made a hand written invitation of two little girls (stick figures) holding hands. I invited her to my home for TEA and gave the time. Because I had a key to her home, I took the dress and invitation over when she wasn't there and laid them out so she would see them when she came home. I fixed the #1 menu and she came at the appointed time. It was such a special time for us. We will never forget it. It was the beginning of a new and very important part of my life. 1 have given many TEAs in my home and because of requests, Rue and Sue's Victorian Armoire and Tea Room was established. By the way The TEA room was in her home. We served two to fifty persons a time. This took place about two times a week and more near holidays. I guess I forgot to tell you that we both had full time employment, so you see, "I don't have time" is not an excuse. Time is a choice.

Take time to be gracious . . .
and enjoy.

Bethelyn Sue Gadbow
Email: bethelynsue@aol.com